My DAD Moved Out
AND LEFT ME

Yvette Wiggins Kinlaw

My Dad Moved Out and Left Me

iUniverse books may be ordered through booksellers or by contacting:

iUniverse
1663 Liberty Drive
Bloomington, IN 47403
www.iuniverse.com
844-349-9409

Because of the dynamic nature of the Internet, any web addresses or links contained in this book may have changed since publication and may no longer be valid. The views expressed in this work are solely those of the author and do not necessarily reflect the views of the publisher, and the publisher hereby disclaims any responsibility for them.

ISBN: 978-1-6632-0439-4 (sc)
ISBN: 978-1-6632-0440-0 (e)

Library of Congress Control Number: 2020912228

Print information available on the last page.

iUniverse rev. date: 08/24/2020

Every day that we wake up, we choose the kind of day we want to have. Life is always about choices. If this book just helps one child, then mission accomplished! I have always tried to teach my children to make good choices in life; they are the heartbeat of my life. I dedicate this book to my children and, especially, my grandchildren, Haley and Quinn. GG loves you very much!

My mom and dad used to take us on vacation every summer. We always did exciting things on our vacations; I liked hiking, swimming, having picnics, and playing games. My dad was so much fun on every trip. He told jokes and played video games with us. My mom packed lots of good snacks for our car trips. She made everyone's favorite sandwiches and had all our favorite drinks. My sister, who is two years younger than I am, always wanted to taste everyone else's sandwich, but I never wanted to share my sandwich.

At the end of every summer, my sister and I would go back to school, my parents would go back to work, and everything would go back to normal. My dad always helped me with my homework, and my mom always helped my sister with her homework. My sister and I loved helping Mom make dinner and set the table. By the time Mom had dinner ready, Dad would come home; he was always happy to see us. We always ate dinner together and talked about everyone's day. My dad told us about his day and made jokes about his commute to and from work. After all our homework was done and bath time was over, my mom always told us a story or read one of our favorite books at bedtime.

When school began at the end of one particular summer, my dad did not always come home for dinner and homework. My mom often looked sad. I asked my mom where Dad was, and she said, "I don't know." After several days of hearing my mom say that, I became sad too! My dad stopped coming home at all, and he was not there in the morning when I got up for school.

After a few weeks, my mom said that she needed to talk to me and my little sister about something very important. I immediately thought that she was going to tell us where Dad was and why he was not at home. I was excited to finally find out about my dad. Mom still looked unhappy, though, so I thought maybe the news was not going to be good.

Mom told us that Dad was not coming back home again. I asked, "Why not?" And then I started crying. Then my sister started crying and ran out of the room.

My mom said, "Your dad and I are getting a divorce."

I asked, "What does that mean?"

She explained that a divorce meant that she and my dad were not going to be living in the same house and that I would not see my dad as much as I used to see him. She said that both she and my dad still loved my sister and me.

I felt like I needed to cry, but I also felt like I needed to be strong for my mom.

I wanted to be strong for my mom, but I wasn't sure I knew how to do that all by myself. So, I did some of the things that I saw my dad doing before he left. I took out the garbage, loaded the dishwasher, and made sure all the doors were locked. At school, my teachers had always said that the school counselor was a good person to talk to about something we were worried about or something that was difficult to talk about. After I talked with my school counselor and explained what was going on at home, I felt happier at school. My mom seemed to be really happy with my help at home, although she still looked sad.

I never cried when I was with my mom, but I did cry when I was alone in my room. I missed my dad, and I didn't know how to handle not having him at home. My dad moved out and left me! I hope I did not do anything bad to make him leave me. I wanted my dad to come back home; if he did, I would be very good. But I felt like there was nothing I could do.

Life was not the same anymore. My mom noticed that no one was happy and laughing anymore. She made an appointment with a family therapist for herself, my sister, and me. The therapist wanted to talk about all our feelings, our thoughts, and our expectations about how our new family looked now. We went to talk to the therapist every week for a couple of months. I looked forward to going to talk with the therapist because I could talk about my dad.

One night after dinner, my mom told us a joke, and we were all laughing and having fun, just like we used to when Dad was with us. We also began talking about Dad and discussing how it was not our fault that he left. I realized that because of the family therapist, we could talk about Dad without crying and being upset. I also realized that Dad did not just leave me—he left *us*!

I learned from our family therapist that it was okay to be sad sometimes. It was also okay to miss my dad, think about him, and continue to love him. The biggest thing that I learned was that it was important to be happy in my life, have friends, and play sports.

Printed in the United States
By Bookmasters